"Kathleen Staudt's *Viriditas* opens our eyes to a luminous world of colors, which then permeates our interior beyond our knowing. It is the 'green of ordinary time,' the 'quick in the root of being,' a vivacity we are blessed to experience, paradoxically, in moments of profound stillness. Staudt invites us into such moments, through poems of quiet love for the world in and around us—both the world and the words being God's gift."

—SOFIA M. STARNES, Virginia poet laureate emerita

"Kathleen Staudt's *Viriditas* is a joyous tribute to nature, green in shoot and bough. In the tradition of Mary Oliver, her poems revel in the seasons closely observed, from the colors and shapes of leaves to the subtle hues of love. Like a wise bee, Staudt confects the honey of contemplation from all the changes and chances of this life."

—BARBARA NEWMAN, professor of English, classics, and history, Northwestern University

"Kathleen Staudt's *Viriditas* is a ribbon of bright light, a gift that invites us to celebrate with her the greening energy of the sacred in poems that open to us like seeds in a soft spring rain. Her poems are an invitation to discover anew how the experiences of being human can daily point us toward the miracles to be found in each moment, 'Breathing in. Breathing out.'"

—MICHAEL GLASER, Maryland poet laureate, 2004–2009

"Whether writing about the changing seasons in her garden or the changing seasons of our lives, for Staudt, every moment is infused with the holy. She has a deep way of listening to the world. Whether writing about her mother's death or family trips to the beach, even her conversations with difficult biblical figures, draw us deeply into her reverence and gratitude for life itself. What a privilege and a pleasure to read these poems."

—EMILY BLAIR STRIBLING, author of *The Mercy of Light*

VIRIDITAS

For Sue
I hope these poems may
inspire you our craft
Kathy

VIRIDITAS

New and Selected Poems

KATHLEEN HENDERSON STAUDT

RESOURCE *Publications* • Eugene, Oregon

VIRIDITAS
New and Selected Poems

Resource Publications
An Imprint of Wipf and Stock Publishers
199 W. 8th Ave., Suite 3
Eugene, OR 97401

www.wipfandstock.com

PAPERBACK ISBN: 978-1-6667-5469-8
HARDCOVER ISBN: 978-1-6667-5470-4
EBOOK ISBN: 978-1-6667-5471-1

04/04/23

Contents

CONTENTS

III | A SOJOURN AT BETHANY

IV | ELEGIES AND EASTER

IV | BEACH WEEK

Preface: About "Viriditas"

The medieval poet and mystic Hildegard of Bingen uses the word *viriditas*, literally translated "green-ness," to name the energy of divine life that she perceives pulsing through all of nature. The word comes from the Latin verb *vireo*, meaning "I am verdant, green; I sprout new growth. I am lively, vigorous." Hildegard's poem beginning "*O viridissima virga, Ave*" is a hymn to the Virgin that can be translated "O greenest branch, hail."[1]Barbara Newman writes that "Viriditas for Hildegard was more than a color; the fresh green that recurs so often in her visions represents the principle of all life, growth and fertility flowing from the life-creating power of God."[2] I shall always be grateful to Hildegard for naming and probing the mystery that many of these poems seek to explore.

I am also grateful to my poet friends Emily Blair Stribling and Hilary Davies for their careful and supportive reading and wise counsel as I was completing this volume.

1. Hildegard of Bingen, *Symphonia*. 2nd ed. trans. Barbara Newman. (Ithaca: Cornell University Press, 1998), 126–7.

2. Barbara Newman. *Sister of Wisdom: St. Hildegard's Theology of the Feminine.* (Berkeley: University of California Press, 1987), 102.

Acknowledgments

"Wondering About Angels" was previously published in *Spiritus*

A version of "Epiphany Walk" was originally published in *Silver Spring Voice*

"Denkmal" originally appeared in *Anglican Theological Review*

"Viriditas I" and "Dust to Dust" originally appeared in *Reformed Journal*

"Reveling" was originally published in *Presence,* the magazine of Spiritual Directors International.

Versions of some poems were previously published in my own volumes, as follows:

From *Annunciations: Poems out of Scripture* (2003: Mellen Poetry Press): "Judgement Day" and "Holy Spirit."

From *Waving Back: Poems of Mothering Life* (Finishing Line Press, 2009): "Autumn *Pange Lingua,*" "Theosis," "Worship" "February Longing," "Reality at the Beach," "The Beach Will Always be Here," "Power Loss," and "Waving Back."

From *Good Places* (Finishing Line Press, 2017): "The Volunteer," "Viriditas III, IV and V," "Presences," "Brood 10 Cicadas:2004," "Epiphany Walk," "Lenten Villanelle,"

I

VIRIDITAS

O viridissima virga, Ave.

—Hildegard of Bingen

the force that through the green fuse drives the flower

—Dylan Thomas

Viriditas

I

The hidden life in me
listens for the voices of the trees.
They are singing, deep beneath
the silver skin of beech trees
sounding roots that hold
the forest floor together,
pulsing upward, lifeblood
from root through trunk and up
to overarching crown.
A song is rising, and sometimes
walking, as today, at winter's end,
watching for the signs, I feel
suddenly, earth's breathing pulse:
Viriditas: It sings in me.

II

St. Patrick's Day, mid-Lent, and I
Am yearning for the green.
I don't know what to wear today.
Nothing goes together
Clashing green sweater and scarf
There are so many shades and hues of green.

I visit the gallery, a Bonnard of spring,
and see how many ways there are of seeing green:
yellows, blues, a bursting gold,
turquoise, violet, blue,
even shadows of deep purple
mixed with lively brushes of chartreuse.

Another painting sees the fullness of green,
the deep shade and dappled sun
of high mid-summer.
Oranges and crimsons mix with rose and green.
Van Gogh has seen what I long to see again.
I must look again when the green returns.

Will I see it then as the artists saw?
I yearn for the chance
to see what I can see:
Is there really violet in the verdant leaves?
There are so many ways of seeing green.

III

Out on the patio, surrounded by green
    after last evening's violent storm
        The air washed clean

I listen to wren song, crow caw, squirrel quarrel
    Wings flutter, tails scurry, birds chirp, peep, scold

Beltway traffic drones and roars
    White noise, half heard beyond the birds
        A low continuo.

Soothed by the cooing mourning doves
    I watch and listen here

On the patio, surrounded by green
    After last evening's violent storm
        The air washed clean

IV

The morning shines on the cherry leaves.
Green and glossy, they shine back
Taking in the light
That is their life.
In the hidden greenness of each cell
Sunlight changes into food
And now the leaves shine back

As one beloved, in the lover's gaze
Gives back the radiance of love received.

V

In caritate let me be
Like a fish in the ocean
Breathing the waves breaking over me

Let me be
Like a bird in the morning
Glistening on air, the sun warm on my wings

Let me be
A woman just passing the change of her life
Resting outside on her patio
Sipping Darjeeling, surrounded by green-ness
Listening to birdsong, soft breeze on her skin.

VI

Some mornings I simply sit
And soak in the green
The tulip tree today stretches out broad limbs
as if to embrace the sky,
its crown now seeded with pale yellow flowers.
Under it the weedy boxelder stands young and gangly,
sun on new shoots, clothed
in classic, bright spring-green.
Sun and shadow shimmer, as if the green,
held in the light, insisted on its color.

I watch and listen to the morning show,
sun and shade, birdsong chorus
soaking in the music of green.

VII

Along suburban roads
Outside of this place of peace,
branches are cut back
to make way for roads and wires.
The tree shapes are determined
not by what they are
but what surrounding busy-ness
has pressured them to be.

But here in open space
each planted tree spreads up and out
freely, rooted in one place
spreading deep beneath the soil,
growing out into the shape
that she was meant to be.

Here in open space
I recognize their names
In distinctive silhouettes:
Pin oak, maple, sycamore.

Let me be
like such a tree
Planted into spaciousness
growing up into the shape
that I was meant to be.

VIII

Viriditas: beneath my feet, along a woodland path
it vibrates in the air in shade
of beech and hickory, an energy
sprung from ancient life still strong,
still flowing in the limbs of all that grows,
feeding the birds and tiny crawling things,
singing forth in dim cicada swell
and in the song of crickets and tree frogs.
I breathe it in through sandaled feet
Summer. Green.

IX

Late August: remember
how the leaves laugh in the morning breeze
before the midday heat.
How cicada song swells
breathing in the quiet, breathing out a scratchy song
breathing. In and out.

Remember the varieties of green:
Weed-trees, sparse and bright
Maple spreading, flat green, sunlit
The tulip leaves darkening
spots of yellow starting to appear.

Cicadas' song swells on the breath of morning,
evergreens still in steady shade.
Remember this, when winter comes
and they alone are holding
the green that plays and sings in everything today.

X

The tulip trees that spread
Above the neighborhood
Are just beginning, now, their autumn change

Still green, but coppery
with just a hint of gold
The gold that soon will cover everything

Like salt and pepper grey
In an old friend's dark hair
Heralding the mysteries of age

Rooted in long living
Soon to be transformed
All over, into silver that will shine.

Presences

Sometimes, like a gift from the hidden world
A rare bird appears in my back yard
Simply, without fanfare,
As if it knew the place, yet belonged eternally
In the other world I glimpse
Just over the patio wall.

Like the goldfinch who arrived today,
Splendid among sparrows,
Perched there on the feeder
Just long enough for me to see
His glorious yellow-gold.

Or the family of owlets I heard screeching one evening
Just beyond the fence
And glimpsed in a holy moment:

A fledgling lumbered, shrieked and flapped
While its mother watched
Strong and serene, from her high perch
As if she were a guardian spirit
Always present, rarely seen.
Then both took off and disappeared
Back into the green.

From my patio I witnessed
Their rushings of white wings.

Brood 10 Cicadas: 2004

We can't avoid them when they come,
    a plague, some say
    of ugly bugs and deafening noise.
They dive-bomb on our picnics, die
    on patios and walks
    in piles of crunching wings.
Their fleeting lives remind us of the fleetingness of ours.

But as for me, I love their treetop wedding song
    They harmonize and whistle: *Wowwowwowwowwow*
I love to see their blunderbussy bodies whirligig
    on lacy wings, like fledgling angels practicing for heaven
They celebrate their lives in sussurating song,
    Breeding and dying, they promise a return
mysterious yet predictable, in seventeen years.

Who knows where I will be, or on what side of life
    the next time they are here.

I'm glad I have not missed them this time.

Brood Ten Cicadas: 2021

Cicada shout returns after seventeen years.
And we are still here.
A rushing spring of sound surrounds suburban yards
and parks and everywhere fill with loud presence.
For once the beltway noise is drowned
By nature's song.

As if the hidden energy
That breathes always through green and growing things
Took flesh, and flew
On lacy wings, with bright red eyes

Emerging from the depths to give
A feast of sound, banquet for beasts and birds
And bodies rising to the tops of trees
to fill the long June days with waves of song.

Traveling God's Green Earth

Here on my porch, just past the summer solstice
I notice the weed trees, the wild grape and berry vines
that soon would cover everything
Without my steady care.

I remember tended gardens of places far away,
all over God's green earth:
Lugano by the lake, where glossy magnolias
and stripey palms mingle with a plane tree canopy
and tall pruned cypress, in patterns that delight
the work of an artist's love.

Around the world, I meet the artistry
of gardeners and farmers, all those loving makers,
who shape the planet's growing things and know
the graces of that life
I celebrate and breathe their holy work.

Valentine's Day Down Under

In the Royal Botanic gardens, where green is everywhere,
the grand oaks transplanted from the north are in full leaf.
I recognize familiar shapes of maple, birch and elm,
but here they are filled with strange bird voices.
Silvery gum and palm and eucalyptus
mix with pine and cypress, and a lawn,
bright green, seems unearned abundance here.
This is a summer whose spring I missed,
whose fall I will not see.
I gaze on the mature and gorgeous green evoked
by words like "summer morning," "mid-July." But here
The words for this are "February:" "Valentine's Day,"
reminding me how far from home we are.

Lugano

When we have left, we will hardly believe
That we were here: the quiet breathing breeze
cool under north Italian sun. And clouds
rising from lake to mountains, to unveil
the clearest sky, and unconditioned mountain air.
I rest on the veranda of this splendid old hotel,
wrought iron railings, shuttered casement, old world cornices
perched on the edge of Lake Lugano. Why a poem,
I wonder: how do I hope to capture here
the quiet restfulness, unhurried pace.
I sip a creamy cappuccino, watch
the sparrows hop, table to table, rest
and watch the morning breeze rustle the palms
and brush my skin, as morning warms and brightens.

Late afternoon. I watch the way the light
has turned the lake to nearly turquoise blue
No: not turquoise exactly—but more blue
than aqua, more green than violet.
Just gazing at the water gives a sense
of blue serenity, held round by sandstone cliffs
and forested slopes, up from the lake
to high meadows and villages, and churches perched
atop the highest bluffs. By the water, people stroll
Along green avenues of plane tree shade
as palm fronds fan in an offshore breeze.
The afternoon stretches out to solstice-light.
As life slows, breathing the mountain air of Lake
Lugano, on a summer afternoon.

Patrishow, Wales

The quiet is alive
in the stones of this Welsh churchyard
and in the church of Patrishow.

This was a place of pilgrimage for you.
When you were facing your life's end,
you gave our friend a tiny cross to carry
back across the ocean to this place.

She has brought me to where she laid it, a token
joining your spirit to this country that you loved.

I have come now to lay down the heavy memory
you shared with me, from your last visit here.
Was it really in this place, of green hills and flowing stream
that darkness fell for you, so finally?
The bottom dropped out, you said, of all that had sustained you
there on the threshold
of your last, hardest journey.
Was it then, you wondered, that the final sickness came?

A pilgrim now, I stand before the holy well you loved,
dark stone, surrounding green
with niches full of tokens
from pilgrims to this place.
I look for your cross,
and I listen to the stream.

The saints, alive in Celtic lands, whisper
we are here—here in this place. We are here: hear:
I hope that is your voice I hear singing among them
here, beside the holy well
below the old stone church
nestled in these rounded hills
at Patrishow.

St. Deiniol's Churchyard, Hawarden, Wales

The quick in the root of being
pulses the lime leaves, fading now to yellow,
that shade the wooded path
sings in the weeds that grow between the rocks
on castle walls,
stalks of dusty green with feathered leaves.

The quick in the root of being
takes root in this silent churchyard
with its stones of grey and brown
shadowed by the quiet church
and shading ever-greens

enfolds us at the quiet altar here,
embroidered with the green of ordinary time.
In silence, we receive the prayer
that makes us whole again.

Hot April

That year, April's heat wave cheated us of spring.
We sprinted through the early growing time, when redbud
and dogwood slowly peep out, and half-grown
leaf buds scatter yellow gold along spindly limbs. Today
untimely heat has burst the buds, forced open tiny leaves.

A few wild dogwoods bloom, white echoes of spring,
the lacy season, when every tree and branch in bud
holds promise. But vines and poison ivy have already grown
up the tulip poplar trunks. High treetops, wispy yesterday
thicken green already. The sky fills up with leaves.

Arriving out of season, summer rushes past the spring,
spreads with the vines that cover shrubbery and sumac scrub. No
    bud
adds sudden color. Dusty green has overgrown
everything already, like leggy weeds in August, late on a hot day
wilting at the playground's edges, after the last child leaves.

Autumn Pange Lingua

Just days ago, the sky beamed through
Rifts in a fluttering canopy
    Of tulip-yellow leaves.
A comfortable place,
    Where leaves rustled, birds cried out
And everything was bathed
    In autumnal mother-light.
Suddenly, today, it is the dying season.
Broken places
    show unconcealed scars
Where once were sturdy poplar-pillars
    Holding back the sky.

Today that sky is nearer, pushing down grey haze
    Between the cowering branches.
In eerie, whitening light, birds and trees fall silent:
    A freezing breeze will be rising soon.
But underfoot, the solid ground thickens yellow
    Carpeted in crackling, gorgeous piles of gold.
And children's swishing feet
    Make a joyful noise.
We have come here to play—
    To make the growing leaf-pile crunch
        To run and shout, fall and rustle, toss leaf-rain, and laugh.
So sheltered, less and less, from the weight of the opening sky,
    We play among the treasures of the dying, living wood.

Elegy: The Tulip Poplar

Mid-pandemic season, after violent summer storms
We woke to the whine of chain saws.

Helplessly we watched, and then could watch no longer
as branch by branch, the crown of leaves
that once had formed the canopy of our familiar sky
tumbled to earth, until only a trunk
stood just below our view from the high deck.

Nothing to be done: it seems it stood too close
beside our neighbor's house.
He felt there was no other choice
except to hack and hew.
I saw the stump that has remained:
wide, deep-rooted still, but rotted at the core.

But that tree was my companion, through the changing of life's
    seasons.
In spring, high yellow flowers, deep shade all through the
    summer.
Its bare limbs studded with brown leaf pods
Held, all winter long, assurances of spring.

The trees now left behind may welcome
longer hours of sun.
But oh, the empty space now left
in our familiar sky!

The Volunteer

The tree sprang up, a volunteer
after we lost the shade
Of the oak tree that came down.
It grew out of a thicket
in a corner of the yard
during the busy years when we
were not paying attention.
Then suddenly one spring, at cherry blossom time
the yard filled up with blooms.

Never invited, fed or tended,
now the upstart cherry tree
Spreads above the house
offering its summer shade
beyond the patio wall.

In June its fruits draw birds
who stay to nest and grow.
All summer long its glossy leaves
shelter hidden songs.

In August and September, as the cricket-song begins,
the cherry leaves are deepening to early autumn green,
then turning yellow, one by one, they drift to the earth
early heralds of the season's turn.

In winter, snow and icy drops along its naked limbs
expose the gangly shape of a tangled, weedy tree.
It branches without symmetry, unlovely, growing free.
We never would have chosen it or planted it there
yet in February light, its bark shines silver-bronze
reminding us of unsought gifts
that bring us what we need.
Unplanted, untended, steadily there:
The grace that volunteers.

II

SHOWINGS AND PRESENCES

Wondering About Angels

*"Thou when thou prayest, enter into thy closet—
and shut the door."
Christ said Shut, and He meant Shut."*

—EVELYN UNDERHILL

What is it about angels, I wonder, on retreat.
And I begin to hear a wordless reply.
They block and close the door I cannot shut myself.
As soon as I consent, they gather gently,
Hold me in clear, desiring, gentle light
All the light I ever wanted. All there is.
Rest here, their voices whisper:
Stay, they say.
Whatever it was that was pulling me away
They have covered with their wings.
Stay here, they say.
The one you love has more for you.
Stay here, and shut the door, they say.

Arriving

I turn off the news on the radio
Head north on 29
toward open space

Noticing along the way
how bare trees trace
their lacy patterns on the winter sky

Soon, bright fields between the shopping malls
gleam in January sun.
Gnarled, persistent fruit trees stand in meadows, strong.

Overhead a starling murmuration pulses
and in the shining winter woods along the drive,
shimmering beech leaves tremble in sparse light

Arriving, I will go and see
What is moving them
What is inviting me.

Epiphany Walk

O rest beside the weary road
And hear the angels sing.

The angels are singing all the time. I can hear them
when dry leaves rustle where I thought the woods were bare.
It is an endless love song they are singing: I can see this
on breathless winter afternoons, among these silver trees.

Parchment-crisp, the beech leaves clinging to these boughs
are white as angel wings. And as the angels stand (they say)
in awestruck adoration, close to the heart of Love,
so these leaf-wings quiver, tuned to a lover's touch.
I have watched them shiver, even when the air seems still.
They whisper as with longing. desiring, desired.

The longest leaves have curled into angel trumpet forms
ready to give voice to the rising breeze.
As it whistles through them, they shake, stand, rustle
sounding through the silence a winter song of praise.

Lenten Villanelle

It seems too soon to let the winter go
The season turns, but still I want to stay
Something is stirring, deep beneath the snow.

The barren landscape beckons me to slow
My walking, notice hues of gray.
It seems too soon to let the winter go.

The grey of beech bark gives a silvery glow
As clinging dry leaves rustle, shine and play
Something is taking root beneath the snow

Days lengthen, and the light begins to grow
More springlike. In the holly, robins play
It seems too soon to let the winter go.

The early signs of life emerge now. Slow
Forsythia buds and snowdrops want to say:
Something is stirring, deep beneath the snow.

In winter's bareness, words have space to grow.
I'll welcome spring's abundance, But today
It seems too soon to let the winter go
Something is taking root, and stirring, deep beneath the snow.

Adelynrood: the Marsh at South Byfield

Cattails and tall grasses bend,
watered deep down
rooted and resilient
in the hidden breeze.

Behind each row of tightly woven grass, another rises,
row upon row, to the river's bend
too dense, too tall for me to enter,
The sun too bright, the mud too deep for me.

But in among the grasses, winged creatures bring tidings.
Crickets trill. Tree swallows swoop and dance.
Their tails flash white as they ride the steady wind.

A goldfinch rests on a cattail just beside me.
his feathers brighten the morning.
Now with scooping flight
he flies ahead of me, perches and turns,
as if he were beckoning, daring me to come
Come follow further, deeper in, he seems to call
Come, come and see!

Adelynrood: The Great Cross

. . .what did he do yet other
Riding the Axile Tree?

—David Jones

Through thick bark of ancient trees
and the craggy roots beneath my feet, I feel
the soul-song of the place.
I think of deep roots sounding
soil built up on granite-rock.
Twirring crickets give a shape
to unheard voices, present here.

The earth itself, the trees, and the gardens are alive
with green life pulsing through Creation redeemed.

A tall cross stands here, on a granite bluff.
Rooted and secure, it echoes back
the shapes of the surrounding trees.
Standing at the axis of this place,
it bears the beating heart of everything.
I rest here in the energy of green.

Adelynrood: On San Damiano Porch

This is my favorite time
The quiet of the house in the last hour
Of the Great Silence, just before the bell.
Companions stir, and early risers settle
on porches and in living rooms, with coffee and quiet.
The only sound I hear is the chirping of sparrows
nesting on the porch roof, loud welcome to the day.

A woodpecker here, crow-calls in the distance
join the silent singing of the green
that wraps the old white pine with its five thick trunks
joined as in a dance.
The breeze this morning barely moves: a hot day looms,
and yet the morning air is cool. Leaves barely stir.
Like me and my companions, they breathe in the day,
the sunlight that becomes their food, the air they feed
and the tall, quiet pines, ever-green, and still.

Adelynrood: The Great Silence

The soul's soil
tapped by hidden roots
nourished in underground springs
takes in the rain that falls
on thirsty loam.
The prayer of rain, the rain of prayer
flows and settles down
feeding arms and bodies
spreading green that takes in
the sun's light, makes life
gives back shade, greenness,
thick trunks where sap flows
bark covers, lichens feed,
birds nest, swoop, and sing.

No words but a breathing in
of green-ness and life.
The cross stands here on a once-bare hill,
towered over now by pines,
their many trunks that twist and reach
up to blue-green shade
down to roots that penetrate
deep into the rock.
Rooted reaching breathing green
shade and sun bright now
around the weathering Cross.

Seed-time: An Oracle

This is the seed-time: Be, like the seed, and wait.
When spring rain seeps through the dark loam,
Crack open, release the first tiny shoots.
Let them reach up to drink, grow, drink again.

Feel the rich soil. Crack once more,
And stretch down roots to hold you there.
You will be changed, as the shoots push up toward the sun,
Greeting the birds of the air.

As the seed is lost in growing, reaching, rooting,
So you may not know yourself.
You cannot foresee the fruit or the flower.
Only be, like the seed, and wait.

This Grasshopper

"who made the grasshopper?
this grasshopper, I mean."

—MARY OLIVER

The one I met this morning in the outdoor labyrinth
She stopped me in my tracks with her delicate jump
So that I squatted down to see her close
My giant knees mirroring her bent rear legs, at rest
She grazed on a reddening wild strawberry leaf
Her threadlike forelegs worked, her red rear legs reflecting
The color of the leaf on which she sat.
Then she must have seen me, with her many eyes
She froze, no doubt for safety
I must have seemed gigantic to her, incomprehensible.
Even if her stillness was born of fear or awe
It was a gift to me,
For I could see her whole: strong legs and agile jaw at rest
I marveled at the process, the millennia of making
To create these eyes, these legs, these graceful wings.
I wonder if she knows she is
Beautiful.

The Marsh at South Byfield II

"There's news to be had in the marshes"

—EVELYN UNDERHILL

I return, and in the stillness
The marsh is singing
After rain: no breeze
Brown cattails, purple loosestrife, and tall grasses stand
Utterly still for a long moment
As if all their life is focused
On the deep roots, taking in
The welcome rain that has just come and gone.

Now a whiff of air rustles, and as I walk
Swallows dart and swoop
And in the very place I saw him last
The goldfinch comes to greet me.
We are now old friends
He perches on the tallest reed again,
And turns to welcome me
Home to this rooted life.

Theosis

It was a great idea.
As you proposed your thesis
I saw myself in you:
Serious, scholarly, mother of an only child
Who would not interfere with your work.

You sat in my office and said:
I want to study
Divinization, *Theosis*:
The ancient idea
That we are made like God,
And grow to up to participate
In the Divine Life
And will come at last to see all life
Within God.

You wanted, I remember, to study
that.

Life brought you something different, two years later
When your only child was joined
By newborn twins.
Premature, they struggled into life.
Your voice, bone-weary and quiet with awe,
Told me, on the phone, you had brought them home.

One day, while you were home alone with the babies
I came to your kitchen, bringing food,
The best food I could find
Enough to fill and soothe your stretched, empty body.
Good enough, rich enough, to cheer us both.
The twin babies, calm in swings, slept alongside us
The rhythm of their swings a music surrounding us.
Your kitchen glowed with our eager conversation
As we wove our stories together.

We were writing your thesis then, my dear
Within the mothering life.

The Healing

Bruised head and foot from an icy fall,
I cannot get home on my own tonight.

I am brought to her door, the door that we found
When we saw lights burning against the snowy darkness
In windows of a house with many rooms.

In her white robe, she greets us at the door
Receives from my companion the heavy bags I carried.

Her quick eye notes
The weight that went down with me when I fell.
Come in, she says. We'll leave this baggage here.

But I begin to panic as I hobble up the steps
Foot aching, head throbbing, shaking with shock.

I think of where I am expected, who will miss me if I stay.
Strands that bind my life together
Unravel, like raw nerve endings, dangling.

I clutch at the cell phone, to rearrange and cancel
the pieces of my life.

She watches from her rocking chair
Talks me through my calendar

Holding the skein for me, until I have knitted up
A fabric that will hold without my thread.

In the room prepared for me I barely notice
Pillows piled high, exactly where I need them
Ice where I am swollen, blankets where I'm cold.

At last I put on the nightgown she provided,
Clean white flannel against my shivering skin.
Her hands rest on my forehead and I receive
The warmth of her strong prayer.

She leaves me then to unencumbered silence, where
Surrendering, in snowlit solitude, I rest.

Holy Spirit

She came to meet me,
Beautiful and strong, and surging with desire:
"What do you want?" she asked me, a twinkle in her eye.
And timidly, I whispered: More.
A little more of this, please:
This springing-up of life, this beckoning mystery.
I want to enter more of it
Even the mud and mess.
More, I would like more, I whispered,
Then drew back.
But perhaps I want too much? I asked.
Am I too greedy?

HA! She shouted,
And her laughter boomed around me.
Look at you!
So drawn and self-controlled
You are
An anorexic at a banquet!
Come, and taste, and eat.
And when you've fattened up a bit,
I'll teach you how to dance!

And stretching out a spindly arm,
I reached for her rich fruits,
And began to taste, and eat.

Icon Writer

What would it be like
to be the icon writer
whose brush, in gentle strokes
unveiled these living eyes,

to draw the brush in silence
around the edges, and to see emerge
the tender eyes
open to mystery.

To find within this artistry
the One who gazes out on me
and draws my gazing home?

Worship

She cannot really say what this is, but only
That she has put into it
Some of her favorite things:
    A special shade of violet-red,
        A bumpy line from a fat yellow crayon;
            A face, her own, in blue, her favorite color;
                A circle, firmly traced in black;
                    Two red and turquoise stickers, dug out of a drawer.

She can't, or won't say what it is,
But she knows
It is *beauty-ful*

Beauty for me:
    the small head bent in deep attention,
        fist clutching pen,
            and her laughter at the sound that felt-tip markers make
                Pounding on paper, spewing dots of color everywhere.

And beautiful her words
    as she places her creation
        into my hands.

This is for you, she says,
Write it, a blessing:
For you, from me,
With love.

The Names of God

I saw a bumper sticker about the names of God
God is not a Boy's Name, it said.
Driving the carpool, I read it aloud.
The young theologians in their booster seats
Discussed the implications of these words.

Of course it's not a boy's name. But does that mean
God is a girl's name? This cannot be so, he said.
And she: maybe it's a boy's name *and* a girl's name
I know, says he: Maybe God has two heads
A boy's head and a girl's head. And maybe those two heads
Talk to one another all the time, just like we do.

But God cannot be only a boy and a girl, they say
God must have many heads, all talking to each other
One body but many heads, and faces, arms, and hands
And every head and every face has its own name
The way that every person in the world
Has a special name.

Their hydra-headed God was sounding monstrous to me
But they were rejoicing, as good theologians do.
Boy's name, Girl's name could not begin to cover
The mystery and delight of their imagining.

I drove along and listened, and tried to contemplate
A God with a face for any name imagined

II | SHOWINGS AND PRESENCES

Beyond all words, beyond all naming
Knowing us each by name.

Rumi's Elephant

(for Kate)

In my dream, I wanted simply
to put my hands on the elephant.
It didn't matter where.
I wanted to be in its enormous presence
simply resting there.

In my dream
I was with a theologian friend
and both of us were silent:
the hugeness in the room
beyond our naming.

Reveling

(for Stephen)

Prayer, Teresa said, will finally be
A simple conversation between friends.
Beyond the drama and the wilderness
The dry places and the upwelling springs
At last, or intermittently, we settle
To daily conversation. That is all

And sometimes, as today, the conversation
Lapses. Nothing, really, now, to say
And even though the silence might appear
To be an invitation into some
Dramatic mystic moment, it is not
Exactly that. Rather, a simple reveling:
Contentment without content: resting in
The quiet being-here that long love brings

III

A SOJOURN AT BETHANY

Luke 10: 38–42

John 11:1–44

Jesus in the House of Martha and Mary

*(A Painting at Bon Secours Retreat
Center, Marriottsville MD)*

Ernestine Foskey, a Sister of Charity
painted and signed this in 1919.
Martha, in the background
dressed in muted pinks and greens
lays out candles, wine with fruit, a simple meal.
Soft sun, a mountain landscape show
through stuccoed roman arches
windows of her quiet, hospitable home.

And here in the foreground
all lines pointing to them,
Jesus and Mary sit, absorbed
in passionate conversation.
She, not submissive on the floor, but seated, facing him.
Her chair is draped in royal blue and gold, her hands
are folded as in prayer.
She listens as he speaks, and he
attends to her: their eyes
fixed on one another.

Lost in their learning, glad to be heard,
he is raising his hand in a teacher's gesture
And she, in contemplation, takes in his words, his voice,

his every gesture, all of him, heart and mind, and he
all of her.

Making, teaching, listening:
The three figures form
a homely trinity

My sister, Ernestine
has made an icon here
of the disciple I desire to be.

Bethany Walk (John 11:1–44)

I

Walking, I follow
the path along the woodland's edge
out into open meadow and a gravel road.
I do not know where it will lead
I walk. I follow.

Walking, I remember Thomas and his friends
walking with Jesus back to Bethany.
Danger awaits him.
He knows it: but the death
of his beloved friend, and sisters to console
call him back. He walks on
toward the place that threatened him
following the road.

"Let us go with him," Thomas mutters, grim.
"Let us go, that we may die with him."
Walking, they follow
their beloved friend.
They walk. They love. They follow.

II

Close to Bethany
Martha meets them on the road,
wanting him alone
away from those who fill the house,
mourners, friends and spies.

To her he speaks the words
that sound through all our grieving:
"I am Resurrection. I am
Life," he says
"Do you believe this? Can you trust?"

(Do I believe this?) Martha answered promptly: "Yes."
Thomas and the others: what about them?
Could they share that confidence?

And what comes next? Out of depths of human grief
Trembling, weeping, He calls out:
"Roll away the stone!"

III

"Roll away the stone?"
I walk and wonder,
imagining his voice, loud in the strength of love,
bursting out of him like the thunderclap
of timpani on Easter morning,
opening the tomb.

Lazarus! he calls,
naming the one he loves, "Come forth,"
and the man steps out,
tentative and wondering:
out of the tomb into life.

"I am Resurrection: I am life" he said and says.
It is the claim that gets him killed. It changes everything.
It breaks open the heart of history, and still he asks
"Do you believe?
Can you trust this?"

I carry the rhythm of his question in my walking.
I walk. I love. I follow.

Martha

I have prayed, for days, that you would return to us
And you did not come.
If you had been here, my brother would not have died.
Where were you?
Surely you knew.
Why didn't you come to see us when there was time?

Now you are here.
Too late. And yet,
With you standing right here, my answer is sure
Anger, pain and all.
With you here,
Bigger than life, stronger than death,
I can respond
    In spite of the stench,
    In spite of it being
    Four days later,
    In spite of you not being here
    When we needed you.

In spite of all this, when you stand there and say, "I am
Resurrection. I am life. Do you believe this?"
With you standing right there,
I have
    No other answer.

Jesus and Lazarus

Lazarus, the human friend
guessed your secret
knew you whole
the friend whose love and welcome
made you trust your human heart.
He was your friend
and he died.

Maybe you knew
you could not have trusted yourself.
Would it have been too hard for you
to let him go?
So. You waited
And he died. And you missed it.

So you deserved
his sisters' accusation
first from Martha's anger, then
harder to hear, from her sister Mary,
Weeping at your feet:
"Lord, if you had been here
     my brother would not have died!"

"Where have you laid him?" you asked, with human tears
seeing at last that your friend was really dead
and you had never had the chance to speak your love
or say good-bye.

III | A SOJOURN AT BETHANY

"Come and see," they said, sternly echoing
your own first invitation.
Come and see what death is
You who are the Life
Come and see what human grief is like.

That was when a stone was rolled away
from your own human heart
And you cried out, weeping:
No!
My friend will not be bound by death. I will call him back.
Call him back: unbind him.
Roll away the stone!

Lazarus

Blinded and bound, I am aware of light
I cannot feel or see.
Something, someone is calling me
a voice I know, and that knows me
but I cannot move out.
I'm stuck here,
unable to move hands or feet
or heart.

Unable, or afraid? Or even
ashamed?
I don't want anyone to see
the putrefying flesh beneath these bonds
the stench grown too familiar now to me.
I cannot move for fear that if I do
I will fall, with none to catch me.
I cannot look, or fear what I will see
if light is shone on me.

Safer, simpler, to remain where I am,
slip back to the death that has already claimed me once.
Left alone, as I had thought
I wanted to be. And yet
the dark security of this place
has been unsettled now.
Someone is opening the tomb!

III | A SOJOURN AT BETHANY

Who can unbind me, set me free?
Who will help me now, I wonder as
blinded, bound, I hobble toward the light.

Critical Care

"She won't remember any of this,"
the nurses keep assuring us: I hope they're right.
The sedative will keep her down, and calm
while her body struggles, battered by infection
and her still beloved self rests hidden, yet alive
entangled in tubes and lines.
She will not remember; we will not forget.

But I choose to remember the waking dream, or prayer
Where I have held her, been with her, in silent vigil here
suspended together in a boundary land
between this place and the unknown, promised life
that we have celebrated
in the best of life together, here.

In this threshold place, stilled in quiet darkness
I am half-awake already. She begins to stir.
A voice we recognize calls faintly from a distance:
Roll away the stone!

I cannot tell which way the voice is drawing her—
whether here, into the light of our shared world again,
and the hard and lonely work of healing,
or there, away from me, toward where I cannot follow.
She is rising up now, shedding tubes and bandages
her chafed body growing whole again.

She squeezes my hand and turns from me,

as listening through my tears

I hear that voice out of the growing light call out: "unbind her
now."

Unbind her: set her free!

Life Support

Breathing the rhythm of the respirator
supporting her life, in Critical Care,
doing for her what for now
she cannot do herself.

I breathe with her, steady in and out,
puffing in light streams
the gift of breath: to breathe
in. Breathe out.

Breathe in the love
with my loved one.
Breathe out for now the messiness.

Praying that soon
she will be able
to do this for herself.

A miracle, this life
Breathing in. Breathing out.

Farewell Discourse I (John 14–16)

Walk with me, You say
Walk with me, and listen
To what I have to say
While I am still here
In the flesh, with you,
Where you can still touch me
Hear my ordinary voice:

There is another way to live
I have tried to tell you.
Pay attention, please, to what
my life has said.

I draw my friends around me.
You know my love for you—how much
I want that love to live in you
Bind you to one another
after I am gone:
It will be soon.

There is another way.
I have been trying to tell you.
Walk with me, you say,
here, in this place
where you are now.
You know where I am going:

Know the way.
Whatever lies ahead,
The way is through:
Come. Walk with me.

Resurrection Imagined

Awakened, he peels off
   The graveclothes, wrapped so lovingly
   By mourning friends.
He does not need them now. He is alive, and this belongs
To mortality.

But as he rolls the linens, he remembers conversations,
   Lives that he has touched, lives
   that have touched his own.
Lives that he is leaving now

He folds the shroud, remembering
   the hands that wrapped, the loves that joined his love
   in life, in grief.

Leaving aside the pile of cloth,
   he moves out toward the place
   where the stone had blocked the light

Strong again in body
   he steps out now:
   trusting, loving:
Fully alive.

IV

ELEGIES AND EASTER

When great trees fall
rocks on distant hills shudder

—MAYA ANGELOU

For Mom, Who Lived Until the Day after her Ninety-Second Birthday

For your ninetieth birthday, two years ago
You asked for three things:
Let all three daughters come to celebrate.
Let us take a picture
And let us make a foursome, and play some hands of bridge.

And so we came, bearing
News of our lives, of husbands, children, grandchildren
Enough to fill two days of visiting.

We took the picture, all of us
Sharing the same smile
Ninety looking pretty fabulous.

And let it not be forgotten:
We played those hands of bridge
Remembering most of the rules you had taught us
We played and let it not
Be forgotten: at 90, you won
That 700-rubber of bridge!

Walking I

The day we learned you had left us for good
I went for a walk at noon in silver woods
To begin to see what the world is like
Without you in it.

Bright springlike February light shone bright
On silvery beeches and parchment leaves
And branches of pale sycamores
Radiant, leafless white

Walking, I recalled
How it was you who taught me
to name the trees by shape of leaves.
There are no leaves today.

Coloring

"Periwinkle" names this shade of blue
That washes the sky today
An early word I learned to read
On the crayons in the big Crayola box

Silver—sepia—ivory
The colors I could use today
to trace these barely budding trees
Shining on the threshold
Of my first spring without you.

Walking II

Now I tread the trail I walked two weeks ago
Noticing how many
great trees have fallen
How fungi and mushrooms grow on decomposing bark
And microscopic living things, teeming out of sight
Begin the process that returns
The tree's life to the soil

I remember as I walk
A sixth grade science class
Each of us assigned a rotten log to survey, day by day
You, both mom and teacher's aide
shared your guidebook with us
Identifying lichens, fungi, ferns and mushrooms
Outcroppings of that hidden, always-active life
That recycles the forest out of death

Two weeks out, these woods now speak to me
Of early years together, years I had forgotten
You, young mother, Girl Scout leader,
Directing the day camp where we spent our early summers
Remembering those days learning suburban woods,
I walk now, without you,
Waiting for the leaves.

Dust to Dust

No one else wanted the old hoover
So I took it, added to a mover's load
Of furniture and memories inherited
The last time you downsized.

No harm, I thought, in keeping
An extra for the basement.
But after all, it stood unused
Until this time of quarantine
When I was home to notice how the dust built up.

Unzipping the case, I found
The bag was nearly full
Loaded with the dust
of the last home you lived in on your own
Eight years ago.

When this dust was collected, you were still alive. Now
Your ashes rest on my sister's closet shelf
Wrapped in your favorite shawl
Waiting out a pandemic before a burial gathering.

I take out the bag and fold it for the trash
Pausing as I hold in my hands
This dust from a completed life
Ashes to ashes, we say. Dust to dust.

Pandemic Spring: Walking

We stay at home these days, and keep our social distance
But on our daily walks, we breathe in gladly
The steady pushing out of life's return.

These April afternoons, walking in the neighborhood
Everything speaks to me of you:
Hedges of red azalea in my neighbors' yards
Recall the bright red blooms right next to our front door.
Deep purple bearded iris, budding now
Echo those that grew along the sun-washed driveway
Of my childhood home. I learned early the word
You used to exclaim:
Look at that gorgeous *rhododendron!*

The dogwood out in front, planted soon after my birth
Bloomed white with generous blossoms like these here.
Cherry trees remind me of the flowering apple tree we climbed
And how, along the split-rail fence, all summer long
Riots of bright roses bloomed,
Like the ones that have opened up today
Bright red, beside my own front door.

Meanwhile

Day by day, the branches
Grow greener. Meanwhile
The red maples have put on
Their russet springtime veils.
The cardinals grow redder by the day.
Their courting calls resound.
Lenten roses drape their silken flowers
And daffodils bloom now by the pink magnolia tree

The Purple Hat

The last time I visited
I brought a knitting project
Knowing we would have a lot of time to sit and talk.
I was copying a pattern from a hat I'd bought
Using a purple chenille yarn
Left over from a long-abandoned project that had sat
Unused and tangled up for years.

So as we talked, and as I knitted,
You took up the task of untangling the skeins
Separating strands to be rolled back up
Into neat and usable balls.

I was in full experimental mode,
knitting up a pattern that was new to me.
I remember how eager you were, in those three days
Of our visiting and talking, to see me finish up
This project we had started together. We both knew
There would not be another chance for this.

Passage

You stayed with us until
You couldn't anymore.
We knew you did not want to leave
Sending birthday wishes
and unspoken good-byes.

I wonder what that time of passage was like.
Did you consent at last, slip willingly
Into long sleep?
Or did you expect to wake up as usual
To aching body and sapped energy
Wondering if getting up again would be worth
The effort it had become
in those last months.

I want to imagine you awakening
From hospital bed to a body whole again
To a fullness face to face
Of all the love that you have known,
Amplified beyond imagining
Love for which our grieving, missing you
Is but a tiny foretaste.
This is the hope we bear, in grieving time.

Walking III

Now we have come all the way through winter's end
And nearly all of spring, the solstice near
Moving into high midsummer. As I walk
I am taken back to camp, those weeks of daily summer life
Joyfully living among trees.

I never got to show you these mid-Atlantic woods.
These southerly trees I have come to love:
Crape myrtle, sycamore, among the oaks and tulip poplars
Take the place for me now of birches, lilacs, apple trees
Of our New England Junes.

You would disapprove of extended mourning.
You would roll your eyes and say: get on with your life.
And yes, the grieving shifts sometimes, from hollow aching
To a quiet breathing in of memory and life
The life we all belong to, have belonged to all the while
The love that sings and breathes among these green leaves.

Farewell Discourse II (John 14: 1–3)

Beloved, know this
A part of me is always here with you
Only
It is a part of me
You cannot see.
And beloved, know this:
I expect
I will see you
Again.

A Corker of A Day

"A corker of a day," you used to say
On days like this—late summer, early fall
Or fresh, bright mornings in Maine or Colorado:
A day to be outdoors,
Breathe in clear air,
Admire a shining sky and lively trees
That startle with their beauty:
Early-reddening maples,
Tall, cool pines on granite mountain rocks
Or quiet oak trees, deepening green, alive with hidden song.

I doubt I ever said these words aloud, myself.
They were your own; now they live on in me.
Today, when for a moment I forgot
How you've been gone now for so many years,
I spoke them out, and longed to turn to you, and say
Look, Dad. Isn't this
A corker of a day!

Easter Memory (Luke 24:5)

The spring or summer after you died
I drove north on 95 to be with Mom
and stopped off at Noroton Church
The church where we were raised, singing of faith and hope
and learned of race, and protest, and practiced justice work
The church whose "fellowship hall" welcomed
Girl scouts, choirs, and youth groups
Where more than once a high school band
called "Creepin'Jesus"
played rock music for a teenage dance.

The church where I remember
Sitting in the balcony, one Easter Day
wearing the new green and golden dress I'd sewn myself
and catching, for a moment, amid the routine joy
the shattering wonder of what we proclaimed.
The preacher's text, that morning:
"Why do you seek
The living among the dead?"
What do you cling to, even when
Something altogether new is offered here?

Now, sitting in the parking lot
of that same church
I remembered your times of faith-filled service here,
Elder and teacher both in wisdom and role,
our simple, busy life in this town, moments I cling to.

They are gone: dead now, as I know
You are, too.

And the preacher's words returned
As I heard them here:
Why do you seek the living among the dead?
From the white steeple and red brick tower,
The words enter my heart again, and my tears
remind me again: you are no longer here
Yet somehow, in the mystery, living, you remain.

I turn the key and leave this parking lot
And with lightened heart
Head back up 95.

Pandemic Triduum: Holy Thursday 2020

"I have longed to drink this cup with you"
Says the One whose mandate is to love
Gathering with friends around a festive table
(A practice now forbidden in these times
When social touch is poison, and the way
We best love one another is to stay apart).

The symbols of this day held in our hearts
Forbidden, in this season, to our bodies.
We cannot drink the wine and share the bread
We cannot pour warm water over feet, and dry them gently
The altar is already stripped of all
We treasured in our life, now borne away.
Our quiet vigil in the emptiness
The symbol that contains our love, today.

Pandemic Triduum: Good Friday 2020

The symbols that contain our love today
Bare, lonely crossbeams, water, wood and blood
Hymn lyrics that we cannot sing together
Invite us now to die into a strange new life.

Wondrous the word repeated in our song
What wondrous love is this, my puzzled soul
Now asks, feeling the weight of loss
Invited to an opening of heart
That *washes all our sins and grief away*
That can receive a suffering born of love
Stronger than grief or death. I stand, survey
And hope to offer back *my life, my all.*

Pandemic Triduum: Holy Saturday 2020

I offer back my love, my life, my all
In time of mourning, in the incongruous sun
Of morning after death brought in the night.
All scattered to our homes, we cannot meet
For burial, or vigil by the tomb
All scattered to our homes, tonight's new fire
Must burn remotely, and by faith, not sight.
Rejoice! The new fire sings of victory
The light shines in the darkness, distantly
We claim the promise, while it is still dark.

While it is Still Dark (John 20:1)

I wait for light
Praying in darkness
for all I cannot know,
mend or understand,
held in this dark love.

While it is still dark
an elusive presence
calls my heart,
restless as the light
is long in coming.

Into the darkness, an old chant comes:
Wait for the Lord:
keep watch, take heart:
Waiting for light. While it is still dark.

Easter Mourning 2020

While it is still dark, the empty tomb.
Without an explanation, opens up
And everything is changed and quiet hope
Begins to dawn in me. I go to walk
In freedom through the neighborhood
On this spring morning when the blossoming
Of dogwoods, redbuds, tulips overwhelms
With beauty of a spring oblivious
To all our human sadness. Gardeners
Are out in their own yards, preparing soil
And sowing seeds that bode a better time
When gathering to grieve, we may rejoice.

Pentecost 2020: Calling Their Names

The feast of Pentecost, and tongues of flame
Burn in hot, angry love for murdered lives.
Names of loved ones who mattered, brutalized
Are called in love and grief, with gathering crowds.

Beyond the flames of love burn furious flames
Of rage consumed in looting and in fire
While riot gear and anarchy assert
The whiteness of enduring violent power.

In tongues of living love and grief they call
The names of people known and loved: Breonna—Ahmaud
George, Trayvon. . . the list too long, killings
Too common, but we call the names we can.

Melissa, Sandra, Michael, Paul, Laquan. . .
The flames of Spirit blowing as a wind
Ask with the poet now: how many deaths
Until we know: that too many have died?

The Spirit burns in rage: the list goes on.

Judgment Day

The nightmare returns: It is 1981,
Inauguration Day, and on the television screens
The Good Guys are in. "Today the world is bright," they say.
Now we will be led by People Like Us."
In the glare of celebration, whole neighborhoods dissolve
Off the screen. Invisible. Disappeared.
          '

Walking toward the subway, from where I have been teaching
Young adults who never learned to read in school,
With sudden clarity, I see
Boarded-up houses,
Dazed and aimless men standing on corners.
A grandmother holds a child by one hand,
Dragging a half-full grocery cart.
A broken church marquee proclaims: JOHN 3:16:
AND GOD SO LOVE. .. . .

Though I ride this subway line, under decaying streets,
And come home to this block of shabby walk-ups,
I could blend in with those bright rulers and their wives.
Our apartment here is newly renovated.
My face is white, my clothes are new.
I am a "young professional"
Desirable tenants, we are just passing through.

The housekeeper has been here.
The walls seem whiter than I remembered,

Clean without my labor.
But on the gleaming window frame
A brown cockroach, the size of my thumb
Looks at me.

In this city, such creatures inhabit all our houses.
The rich use chemicals to remove them when they come.
The poor live with them, having no choice.
Reaching for the spray can, I forget for a moment
The colonies of his fellows
Who live within these walls, and under these streets,
And in my neighbors' houses.

Looking back at him,
I decide
Because I can decide
To let him live.

Ash Wednesday 2021

And it is Lent again. Another Lent
of unchosen enclosure. No retreat
into a place of silent hospitality
is possible this year, and so I must
explore alone that storied inner space
that monks have called the cloister of the heart.

Returning to that space, with all my heart
I draw a cleansing breath, and learn anew
that here is space and food and light for me.

A spring of water flows through fertile soil
and silence is so deep and nourishing
that it gives birth to words that do not need
voice to be spoken, but that simply speak
in tongues of steady, all refreshing love.

Restless

Loneliness of disembodied church
mourning the rift exposed

We, the comfortable, survive.
Those who had to work to keep us going

succumbing now to illness and contagion
die more readily, and we at home

don't want to see, but witness, nonetheless,
the suffering of families like our own

What can we do? Surviving, we lament:
Is this the fast we're called to? First to see

Then to repair, whatever way we can
the breach that separates us. So we pray

for hearts transformed and readiness to change
let justice be the cross we bear this Lent.

Pandemic Lent, 2021

Coming to mid Lent
    I pause again
    to pray
And look for signs of spring

The light grows brighter now
    Cardinals
    feathering
With brighter wings, new songs

Within my heart, a blankness
    Not ready to grasp
    hope
Or trust that times will change

Still honoring the rules
    But yearning to step
    out
From danger of contagion

The call to be right
    Where I am
    not
run ahead of time.

More difficult to follow
>But I know
>still
You call me to be here, at prayer.

Coventry: Two Tankas on the Cross of Nails

Charred cross-beams outstretched
Risen from burned out ruins
Bear the prayer: "Forgive"
Open to the sky
Gothic arches sing *Amen.*

Father forgive. Not
Forgive them and not even
Forgive us. No us
and them. Only this: *forgive.*
Sow the seeds of peace.

Denkmal

At the Holocaust memorial in Berlin:
"Denkmal an die gemordeten Juden Europas"

If you walk through here
on your way somewhere else
You will find your way
Suddenly narrowed
Hemmed around by rows of marble slabs
Pillars Monuments *Denkmale*
For the Jews of Europe
Murdered *gemordeten*
The pillars close in and
the cobbled path slants,
Undulates beneath your feet
Walking, you lose
Sense of where you're going

And the monuments
Denkmale Remember now
Go on and on, the paths like one another
And the slabs
Indistinguishable,
Crowd in together;

You don't know, walking through here
Where the path could lead.

You suspect there may be
no way out
So many tall and faceless stones
Like prison bars, like headstones
Monuments: *Denkmale*
Remember now: Denk mal.

Emmaus Poems (Luke 24: 31–32)

I

The airport here in Frankfurt is bright at all hours.
This morning it is full of people, speaking, moving purposefully.
Tall, fair and focused, they pass me by.
I am newly arrived, unsure what time it is,
Knowing only where to go and wait,
and where to wash my face.

On the way, I meet a brown-skinned woman
Short, dressed in black and lace, dragging a lumpy bag.
She sees me seeing her, looks up, and grasps my arm.
"Sao Paolo?" she inquires. She expects me to know.
I meet her eyes and shake my head
"No- no idea what plane."

Then I understand: the ocean she desires to cross,
I have just passed over.
"Sao Paolo—en Brasil?" I ask, in helpless Spanish.
"Si!" she rattles on, in excited Portuguese.
She sees I cannot understand.
But we have met each other.

Turning away, she meets my eye again,
      Raises fingers to her mouth
And blows a gentle kiss

II

The setting is the firehouse, just off the beltway exit
Where late one Easter Eve, driving home from the Great Vigil
I stopped, suddenly stranded, safe, joyful and flat-tired.
Without a spare, I waited for the rescue truck to come.

In my dream, I am at that firehouse
A grand piano stands there, like the one at church
And a soul-friend, my priest from those years, is there with me.

In the dream, I am teaching him a song
We are silly, and laughing, as I sing out loud
With new-found, odd conviction, an old gospel tune:
When the roll is called up yonder, I'll be there, I sing,
When the roll. . . when the roll . . . we sing with giddy joy

Another person lingers in the room with us
Young, in jeans and pony-tail. Smiling in the corner
He listens to our revelry.

The dream-scene vanishes. Waking, I ask
Already knowing: *who was that guy in jeans?*

III

They are waiting for me, with quiet eagerness
In the parking garage I visit all the time
He in his tan jacket, with the plaid lining
From LL Bean, and matching soft-brimmed hat
She stands beside him, wearing
the heather fair-isle sweater she knitted for herself
Both ready to greet me for a routine adventure.
A third person is with them — someone they know well
And want me to know better.

Arriving in my prius, I choose my parking space
self-consciously, knowing that they are watching,
having taught me how to drive, so many years ago.
I drive a little past them to choose an easy space
Where I can park straight on the first try.
I feel them watching fondly, from long habit.

Emerging from the car to go and greet them I know now
I am in a dream: they are long gone from this life.
But their silent presence in this moment has been real.
I wake up calm
and with a gently burning heart.

IV

BEACH WEEK

"far off, a long day's journey
There's a marsh that stretches down to the sea (the sea! the sea!)"

—EVELYN UNDERHILL

February Longing

In windy February gray, late after school
Waiting in a restless carpool line,
I rummage for something in the mini-van's trunk
And breathe in, with a sudden sob, the tangy scent
Of seashore sand and water, clinging to the carpet
Back where no sweeper could reach.
I discover, left behind the seat,
From when this same car
Drove us home from summer,
A perfect scallop shell.

When we found it
It must have been just this time of day:
Late afternoon, the hot sand cooling,
As roselit grey haze softened the sun to blue
Sea light that told us, as the beach was emptying,
We still had hours of daylight left ahead
With no one waiting, nothing to do
But walk along the lapping shore, breathe in salt wind
And search, in the receding tide
For perfect shells.

Reality at the Beach

Just now, there is nothing else in all the world
Except this warm and sifting sand,
Flecked with orange crystal shell-shards,
Flowing from this child's blue shovel.

Filling her yellow pail, she packs and smooths, digs and dumps.
Now she dips her fist into the beach, and spills
A sandpile on her bent-up knee;
Watches, fascinated, as the tingling sandfall flows
Down her ankles, burying her toes.

Around her sounds the steady, solid bass-beat
Of crashing surf against the jutting sand-bars.
The swimmers' shouts. The seagulls' cries.
And through it all
An offshore sea breeze blows her hair and cheeks.

The child leaps up and rolls across the sand,
Down to the edge of the sea
And squealing, leaps
Into my arms.

And there is nothing else in all the world, just now,
Except these sandy arms that cling around my neck,
This salty hair against my cheek,

This scratchy body
And her laughter, mingling
With the sand and the wind and the sea.

The Beach Will Always be Here

Year after year, we learn the waves.
Our children teach us.

First, cautious toddlers play toe-tag.
While further out, waist deep, wriggling children squeal.

Last years' children grow strong, lean bodies,
Strike out for the sandbar, learn to ride the breakers in.

And some years, the wind has turned, and treacherous pounders
Have driven us all back up the shore, to watch in awe.

Year after year, children tumble, crawl, roll, dig,
Stand up, run out, ride in, rest.

When it's time to leave, the youngest ones wail
And we overhear a father, who soothes a mourning child

He says what we all want to believe:
It's OK.
We'll come back:
The beach will always be here.

Power Loss: (Outer Banks, N.C., August 2001)

Sudden dark releases us
From lights that blocked the stars.
Pitch black and heat inside drive us out
Onto the balcony, into strong night breeze.

Black sky, alive with stars, spreads out above us.
Where ancestors found mystery, we track shooting stars.
Our children look for satellites.

Ocean surrounds us
Green and gold fireworks flash from a beach below
Calling out gasps of delight from neighbors' porches.

A few guitar chords sound.
We begin to pick out
Songs we know by heart
    oldies to our kids:

    The answer is
                blowin' in the wind
    Don't think twice,
              It's all right
O   Bla   Dah
        Life goes
On

Waving Back

I remember the summer your body first began to stretch.
We went, just you and I, to a salt pond by the seashore.
You loved it because it was broad and shallow
And you could wade out into it, and leave me behind.

I sat on the shore and watched you,
The growing body in blue stripes.
With every few steps, you would turn to wave
And see me waving back.

The water gets deeper. You stretch out taller,
Swim forward, dive under, look back less.
But my part doesn't change: I watch from the beach.
And when you turn to check, I am still here
Ready to wave back.

Oceanfront

Here
sipping tea,
I listen as the waves roll on the sand
and the sun, veiled in cloud
silvers the ocean's face
and hides again.
I watch and listen, breathe it in
(The sea! The sea!)

Learning to be
fully here:
Doors and windows open
to the sea's continuo,
Never away from the waves' song sounding
rolling onto sand, as the sunrise casts
a ribbon of light too bright to look upon.
Wave sound. Dawn light
(The sea! the sea!)

Six Mornings on the Outer Banks

I

A great blue heron
Still in morning light
surveys the glassy surface of the sound
with sharp attention.
Sometimes he stretches
a graceful neck,
Sometimes as now, crouched over
watches the still water
from that high perch on the osprey platform.
Each time he moves, he holds his motion
still as a yoga pose,
alert and watching
as I have been, watching him
from my perch on this soundside bench,
as in the trees behind me, cicada song swells
this humid morning on the soundside
near the summer's end.

II

Start the day here
        Listen to cicada swell
in wax myrtles and pines
here beside the sound.
Gaze at the grasses and with their seeded tops
        Breathe with cicada chorus
Hear the quiet rumble of strollers and skates
as families walk the weathered boards
Admire the starry leaves of sweet gum, marvel
at the height bayberry grows to
in this southern climate.

Clouds are parting, and the day
which could have gone either way
Opens to pale sky.
Before the day's heat triumphs, breathe
from this place in deep green shade
        rising and falling, the cicadas' song.

III

The surface of the sound is smooth this morning.
Here and there, a paddle board, a kayak,
crabbers at the ends of the pier
move lazily as the day's heat grows.
Here among the pines, the voice of all this greenness
breathes its rounded phrases, cooling down
these southern seaside woodlands, as the day's thick heat
slows the walkers on the boardwalk, slows
all things, except the elusive breeze
against already sweating skin. On the water
a brushing movement spreads as I rest here
Shaded, by the sound, stilled by cicada song.

IV

The bridge back to the mainland
is veiled in cloud today
Watch the heron, osprey, gulls
Walk beside the sound.
Then turn back toward the ocean
For one more timeless day.

V

Just after dawn
we know the sun is up
because a ribbon of pink light
shines across the surface of the sea.
A bank of clouds swells from the horizon
Glows with pink and amethyst.
Ocean surface shimmers, turquoise, rose
And grey mother-of-pearl.
changing every moment.

Broken now by foaming waves, the bright ribbon fades.
Will it burn off? Will there be a storm?

The waves continue with their steady hiss
breaking out in foam.
Morning cloudlight spreads across the surface of the sea.

VI

Ahead of the hurricane
blowing now through Florida,
all things hold their breath.
Cicadas fall silent. Sea grass stills.
The sound surface smooths
except for swirls from breathing crabs.

Now a raindrop, and another, and a mounting breeze.
On the horizon, dark clouds shed their rain,
while here it is still bright, the sky flat white.

Energy gathers with the storm we know will come
later, we hope, after our last day here.
In stillness we watch the not-so-distant clouds.

To Weather a Storm

To stay put, listening from a restless bed
as the ocean grows and rolls, crashing waves against the dunes
as the battering wind
shakes the windows on the ocean front,
throws shingles from the roof and shakes the house.
The maps show it is passing through. The locals say
it will soon end, and calm return.
They say it is the kind of storm that happens:
no need for flight or panic.
But while we are in it,
all we know is the wind
roaring all around us
to show how close we are.
All we can do
is listen to the surf, endure the battering winds
watch for water leaking through,
marvel at the elemental strength
of air and water.
All we can do now
is weather the storm.

Sunrise: Oceanfront

Silent with my friend
On a deck at ocean's edge
We await the rising sun.

We think it may have come already
When the sky has brightened
And the day's thick clouds
are edged with pink and rose

But there is more

The waves intone with a deep, rolling rhythm
And the sea oats, which were waving in an offshore breeze
Now stand still

To the west, a red moon sets
Wind wash and crickets
sound a melody
And now the breeze is rising again.

Yes: there is more

Just when we thought the show was over
Sunrise done, behind the clouds:
A blinding sliver of bright light
Orange—round — appears
Suddenly too bright to look upon

IV | BEACH WEEK

I close my eyes, to feel
The light against my eyelids
Receive the rising breeze against my skin

We can bear to look upon
The ribbon of bright light
Across the ocean's face
But the sun itself, too bright for eyes
Keeps rising, warming, shining

Always, there is more

Notes on the Poems and Epigraphs

In caritate literally means "In love" - but the Latin form of the verb means "in" in the sense of "held in," or "deep within" - in charity, in love.

Pange Lingua is a Latin Hymn to the Cross by Venantius Fortunatus, traditionally sung on Good Friday.

The epigraph to "Wondering About Angels" comes from Evelyn Underhill, *Fruits of the Spirit* (London: A.R. Mowbray Ltd. 1982), 5–6.

The epigraph to "Epiphany Walk" is from the popular carol by Edmund Sears, "It Came Upon the Midnight Clear."

Adelynrood Retreat and Conference Center in Byfield, Massachussetts is the spiritual home of the Society of the Companions of the Holy Cross (schccompanions.org).

The epigraph to "Adelynrood: the Great Cross" is the last line of David Jones's long poem *The Anathemata* (London: Faber and Faber: 1952*).*

The epigraph to "Elegies and Easter" is from Maya Angelou's poem "When Great Trees Fall," in *The Complete Collected Poems of Maya Angelou.* New York: Random House, 1994).

The phrase "*This* grasshopper" comes from Mary Oliver's poem, "The Summer Day," in *New and Selected Poems* (Boston: Beacon Press, 1992).

"The Triduum" refers to the three days in the Christian liturgy that commemorate Christ's Last Supper, Crucifixion and burial, leading up to the celebration of Easter.

The epigraphs to "The Marsh at South Byfield II" and to "Beach Week" are from Evelyn Underhill's early poem "Thought's a Strange Land," in *Theophanies* (London: JM Dent, 1916).

About the Author

An educator, spiritual companion, scholar and retreat leader, Kathleen Henderson Staudt has taught for many years at Virginia Theological Seminary and Wesley Seminary. She is the author of three volumes of poetry and two scholarly studies of the artist and poet David Jones, and was a finalist in the 2021 Paraclete Poetry Competition. Her poetry, essays and reviews have appeared in *Spiritus, Ruminate, Christianity and Literature* the *Anglican Theological Review* and *Presence,* among others.